BRITAIN IN OLD P[

HOVE

JUDY MIDDLETON

SUTTON PUBLISHING LIMITED

Sutton Publishing Limited
Phoenix Mill · Thrupp · Stroud
Gloucestershire · GL5 2BU

First published 1996

Copyright © Judy Middleton, 1996

Cover photographs: *Front*: St Ann's Well
Gardens; *Back*: the bandstand.

British Library Cataloguing in Publication Data
A catalogue record for this book is available from the
British Library.

ISBN 0-7509-1374-6

Typeset in 10/12 Perpetua.
Typesetting and origination by
Sutton Publishing Limited.
Printed in Great Britain by
Ebenezer Baylis, Worcester.

CONTENTS

The staff of Hove Library assembled on the roof garden where the newspapers were set out for the public to read, 1909. Later this area was converted into the Wolseley Library. The two women are cleaners – no females were employed as library assistants until the First World War led to a shortage of young men. The man in the centre is John Lister, Chief Librarian from 1892 until 1935. By 1920 Mr Lister's staff consisted of three men and five women.

INTRODUCTION

In October 1896 an enquiry was held at Hove Town Hall into the application made by Hove District Council to be incorporated as a borough. It is therefore ironic that one hundred years later 1996 should be Hove's last year as a separate borough. The 1896 enquiry lasted four days and most of the influential people in Hove were in favour of including the Vallance estate, the Goldsmid estate and the Stanford estate – the three largest land holdings at Hove. There were 3,758 votes in favour of borough status and only 163 against. However, one of the anti-party was Brighton Town Council, who opposed it on the grounds that a charter of incorporation would prevent them from annexing Hove. In August 1898 Hove was granted a Charter of Incorporation.

The rivalry with Brighton was nothing new of course. It stemmed right back to the days when Brunswick Town was being built. Attempts by Brighton to annexe Hove occurred in 1844, 1854, 1873 and 1876. But Hove had a stalwart champion in James Warnes Howlett. A popular jingle went 'Howlett and Hove/Names almost synonymous/Since Howlett's sharp move/Made Hove autonomous'. But still the rumblings continued and the next flare up was in 1946. Finally in 1994 the government decided that Brighton and Hove should become a Unitary Authority.

HOVE.

Hove's coat of arms was issued by the College of Arms in 1899. The blue cross represents St Andrew, Hove's patron saint, while the gold leg irons are for St Leonard, patron saint of Aldrington. The blue and gold chequers derive from the arms of William de Warenne, while the martlets stand for Sussex. In 1975 the College of Arms pointed out that the coat of arms was not strictly valid since the newly added area of Portslade was not represented.

THE SEA FRONT & THE LAGOON

Edwardian postcards of the sea front lawns showing the 'Peacock Parade', as E.V. Lucas termed it, depict a calm and elegant scene. But the tranquillity belies the early difficulties the authorities experienced in protecting this stretch of coast from the inroads of the sea. Indeed when Brunswick Terrace was being constructed in the 1820s rough weather drove sea water into the foundations of some of the houses. Famous Victorian engineers were called in for advice. Sir Joseph William Bazalgette arrived in the 1860s and recommended a drainage system, while Sir John Coode came in the 1880s and reported that a new sea wall was absolutely essential.

In fact Sir John became somewhat annoyed at the way the Hove Commissioners shuffled their feet over the enormous expense involved and he threatened to pull out altogether. Another winter of bad storms and flooding finally persuaded the commissioners that a sea wall had to be built.

Even if sea water was kept at bay, salt spray regularly scorched the grass which then had to be replaced. For instance, in November 1890 the surveyor reported that a recent gale had destroyed the grass on the south side and it would cost £25 to replace.

It was customary for fashionable people to take a stroll along the Brunswick Lawns after church. It was said that if you wanted a preview of what might be worn at Ascot you only had to look at the Sunday morning church parade at Hove.

The *Brighton Gazette* could not quite see the connection between attendance at church and parading up and down in all your finery. However, a reporter was always despatched to comment on the fashions.

Note the fine hats and dresses worn by the two ladies on the right. The iron railings set in a granite kerb date from 1902 and replaced an old wire fence. The shelters with glazed sides also date from 1902.

Military bands used to play in the shade of a temporary bandstand. Although the 20th Hussars were there in 1906 it seems that the Irish regiments were the most frequent visitors with the 6th (Inniskilling) Dragoons in the 1890s and the 4th (Royal Irish) Dragoon Guards in the years leading up to 1914, by which time at least five military bands were engaged.

In the background can be seen the Alexandra Hotel, the only part of Brunswick Square and Terrace allowed to indulge in commercial activities. It opened as a hotel in 1834, but by the time Prince Metternich stayed there in 1848 it was a private residence. But it did become a hotel again.

This view gives the impression of a very spacious promenade. It was intended to be so as the council forbade carriages, equestrians and cyclists from using it in 1897. But you were allowed to lead your horse across if you intended to bathe him in the sea. The gas lamps date from 1885.

The lawns at the foot of Brunswick Square, before 1906. In that year sixteen additional seats with glazed screens were placed along the promenade. You can see the empty recess to the left of the picture.

An interesting view because while people stroll along on the left, a capstan is being worked on the right to haul a boat up on the beach. In the distance are the new electric lamp standards made by John Every of Lewes, erected in 1923.

The wall seen here was not merely ornamental for it divided the public promenade from the lawns which were for the private use of the people living in the houses opposite. Underneath the Grand Avenue Lawn there was a 29,000 gallon reservoir. Sea water was stored here before being pumped into nearby houses so that people could enjoy a sea water bath at home.

Altogether the private lawns and gardens extended over 18 acres, and all were acquired by a compulsory purchase order instigated by Hove Council in 1947.

A splendid view of both the terraces which made up Queen's Gardens. Unfortunately the first block was demolished in the 1960s. The second block was the Prince's Hotel, where on 22 September 1939 the Supreme War Council of the Allies, including Neville Chamberlain, the prime minister, took lunch.

Although the gardens opposite Queen's Gardens were still private when this view was taken everyone could enjoy the flowers. Note the curved hedge which protected the plants from sea spray and the wattle panels which acted as wind breaks.

An older view of the Queen's Gardens area, but looking west towards Medina Terrace. This postcard was sent in 1909 so the hedges must have been a feature for some years.

Unlike Queen's Gardens, the houses comprising King's Gardens are dissimilar in style – some in red brick, others in more restrained yellow brick. In one of the latter, at 8 King's Gardens, Arthur Sassoon lived from 1883 until 1912 and was visited by Edward VII on several occasions.

On the left are the gardens of Courtenay Terrace. These houses date to the 1830s and were the only properties at the time whose grounds ran down to the sea. But Hove Council wanted to extend the promenade and served a compulsory purchase order. Compensation was disputed, but in 1908 it was settled at £2,363.

This photograph was taken in the late 1930s. Note the open top bus and the beach huts. However, the beach huts are in a position unfamiliar to us today — on the south side of the promenade, thus effectively blocking the sea view from strollers.

From at least the 1880s and probably earlier the area south of Medina Terrace was known as the Quarter Deck. Note the sloping beach in the background – the sea wall was not extended here until 1923, when it stretched from the Medina sea wall to the foot of Fourth Avenue.

A fine view of Courtenay Terrace from the Quarter Deck looking across Medina Lawn. This small garden, known in the last century simply as The Lawn, was purchased from a Mrs Inman in 1852 for the private enjoyment of people living in nearby houses.

Plans for the Medina Esplanade were first mooted in 1888. However, there were complications, such as the bankruptcy of Mr Gallard (owner of the west wall of the Quarter Deck) and the old properties close to the beach at the foot of Sussex Road and Victoria Cottages. It was finally built in 1892 at a total cost (including new groynes) of £11,000.

The whole Medina Esplanade development was dependent on the success of the Medina Baths, which would enable the Hove Commissioners to claw back some of the money expended on the works. The Medina Baths were opened in 1894 with separate swimming baths for men and women and ordinary baths

This part of Hove beach is opposite where the King Alfred stands today. The Medina Baths lasted longer than expected because they were still in use during the Second World War when the new swimming baths had been requisitioned as HMS *King Alfred*, the RNVR training establishment.

The extraordinary house in the left background was called 'Casa Amoena', and the Dowager Duchess of Sutherland was living here in about 1908, when this photograph was taken. The house survived until 1938.

In the background stands the fine block known as St Aubyn's Mansions. Plans by Lainson and Son were approved by Hove Council in 1899 and were designed to accommodate eight flats. However, the residents did not appreciate the proximity of the Medina Baths (which included a laundry) and complained about the smoke.

The coastguard station was yet another obstacle in creating a continuous esplanade. The coastguard station near the foot of Hove Street had been on the site since the 1830s and the land was owned by the Admiralty who refused to be accommodating in the 1880s. It was not until 1894 that the Admiralty agreed to the Battery, Semaphore and Flagstaff being set back to the position seen in this postcard.

The old Medina Esplanade, renamed King's Esplanade in 1909, in the 1930s. Note the bathing tents on the beach and the splendid shelter on the right. It is amusing to recall that in 1898 a petition with 457 signatures was sent to the Works Committee asking for sheltered seats on Medina Esplanade but the committee thought it undesirable to take any action.

A rare view of the miniature railway track which used to operate on No. 1 Western Lawns. It opened in 1928 and survived until 1939. It was owned by Mr F. Russell Hutchinson of Surbiton who built everything himself. The railway ran each summer and takings were donated to the Southern Railway Servants Orphanage.

In 1935 Ernest Latham, an expert surveyor, advised Hove Council that the coastal erosion at west Hove would accelerate and that permanent sea defences should be started as soon as possible. This new sea wall was the result, built to the specifications of the borough surveyor, T.R. Humble.

The sea wall was built of reinforced concrete with flint faced wall. The stepped construction was adopted because it reduced the scouring action at the toe of the wall. The low parapet saved the cost of railings but even so the estimated cost of the project was £29,000.

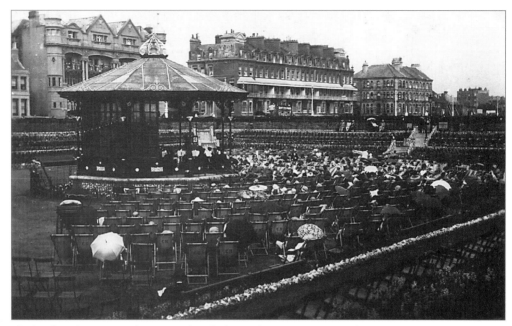

The bandstand was erected in 1911 after the borough surveyor suggested that the putting up and taking down of the temporary bandstand was 'attended with considerable inconvenience'. He chose this site, formerly occupied by bushes in the centre of a lawn, between Walsingham and Carlisle Roads.

The bandstand cost £246 10s 0d and it was not until 1923 that a revolving glazed screen was fitted to it. The first season was opened by the band of the 4th Dragoon Guards and more money was raised there than from the concerts on Brunswick Lawns or St Ann's Well Gardens.

The bandstand was later surrounded by a circle of concrete to make a dance floor. On summer evenings, with a band playing and festoons of electric lights overhead, the bandstand was a romantic place for courting couples. The bandstand was finally demolished in the 1960s.

The Lagoon, seen in about 1908, in its natural state – a fast drying-out pond that had once been a tidal reach of the River Adur. Its history dated back as far as the fourteenth century when the river used to run out to the sea at Aldrington. In 1900 Councillor Nye thought the Lagoon ought to be improved but the council did not think the 'matter sufficiently pressing'.

Work was started on the Lagoon in 1921 and continued for two seasons, providing work for unemployed men. But it ground to a halt in 1923 when the Unemployed Grants Committee refused to sanction more work on the project. The Lagoon as we now know it did not take shape until 1930.

When the Lagoon was created, shrubs, flower beds and a small putting green were also part of the scheme. But salt spray soon knocked that idea on the head and the putting green was moved to a more sheltered spot.

This photograph shows a few toy boats, but the Lagoon was also the venue for serious model yachting events. During the Second World War the Lagoon performed another function – it acted as a training ground in the run-up to D-Day. Tanks which had been made watertight were tested here at night.

A children's playground in the 1930s was a simple affair – a sandpit and a few swings. In the background is the newly opened Caffyn's Garage, now a listed building.

A hard tennis court was talked about on Western Lawns as far back as 1895. When this view was taken in about 1908, bowls and croquet were also played on Western Lawns. During the First World War two of the lawns were cultivated as allotments.

Bowls were first played on the Western Lawns in 1897. Hove Bowling Club was formed in 1896 and the Kingsway Bowling Club in 1925. The new clubhouse was erected for the Kingsway Bowling Club in 1934 and is seen on the left.

ST ANN'S WELL GARDENS

T he name St Ann's Well only dates from the 1880s — before that the area was known as the Wick or the Chalybeate because of its medicinal spring. The word 'chalybeate' means a spring containing iron or minerals. It first became fashionable in the 1750s and later great ladies such as Queen Adelaide, Princess Augusta Sophia as well as Mrs Fitzherbert came to drink the water. The spring was part of the Wick estate whose new owner in 1830 was Sir Isaac Lyon Goldsmid. But visitors were still welcome and the Goldsmid estate leased the gardens — probably the most famous lessee being George Albert Smith, the film pioneer.

Hove had long had its heart set on acquiring the gardens for public enjoyment. The first approach was made in 1885, but Sir Julian Goldsmid wanted £30,000 for 7 acres which was considered far too high. The next serious offer was made in 1906, but it involved a 100 year lease and Hove wanted the freehold. Finally in 1907 Hove Council succeeded in purchasing the 11 acres 32 poles for £10,000 from Mr D'Avigdor Goldsmid who, it was said, could have made more money by selling the land for building purposes. Not every councillor was enthusiastic about the purchase — twenty-three voted in favour and fifteen against.

St Ann's Well Gardens were opened on 23 May 1908 by the Mayor of Hove, Captain A.B.S. Fraser. He is seen here arriving in the carriage with the mayoress and opposite them are Mr Endacott, the Town Clerk and the Revd Prebendary Peacey, vicar of Hove. Sitting on the box seat holding the mace is Mr Fox, the mace bearer.

After unlocking the gates with a ceremonial key, Captain Fraser and his party proceeded to the Well House in front of which a small platform had been erected. Alderman Howlett occupied a prominent seat at the front.

The Well House contained a pump room measuring 32 ft by 19 ft where visitors took the water; the well room was on the ground floor. In 1831 invalids who wanted to come to the chalybeate 'but to whom expense is an object' could be admitted free of charge on production of a medical certificate.

When the borough surveyor examined the Well House he found the west wall was built of rubble about 14 in thick, battened on the inside. It bulged outwards in the centre and some of the rubble was quite loose. But the Well House was a pretty subject for picture postcards.

St Ann's Well became more strait-laced under council ownership. In the days when you had to pay 3*d* to get in (or 6*d* on a Sunday) there was the celebrated gypsy fortune teller, Mrs Lee, in her Romany caravan. There was also the monkey house and ferns, flowers and grapes were on sale from the glass house.

Balloon ascents were another great crowd puller in the old days. In 1894 G.A. Smith managed to attract a crowd of almost 4,000 people to watch Neil Campbell going up in a hot air balloon while the band played. Band performances were one thing which survived.

The old cave, or hermit's cave, was one of the features of the gardens. No doubt stories were related about this folly in a similar way to the charming fable concocted in the 1880s about the origin of the well, which supposedly stemmed from tears shed by Lady Ann for her slain lover.

The hermit's cave can be seen on the left with steps up the side. For many years the gardens were advertised as '6 acres of refreshing foliage and shady walks'. Indeed it was a standard joke that all the trees in Hove were in one place – St Ann's Well Gardens.

In the 1820s the Chalybeate had plantations of firs protecting it on the north and west sides while the south side held open views of cornfields and meadows stretching down to the sea. In 1882 the *Brighton Gazette* wrote that it was 'pleasantly shaded in summer time by trees and rendered additionally delightful by the carolling of birds'.

This romantic postcard depicts the Chalybeate as a veritable waterfall and obviously owes something to the artist's touch. A writer of 1824 described the water as 'soft, not unpleasingly martial and temperate in point of heat'. In its heyday the spring produced something like 300 gallons per day, but by the 1930s it had dried up because of the sinking of an artesian well nearby.

Perhaps the pond was constructed to continue the historical link with water. In the background can be glimpsed some of the thirty-nine decorated vases lining the pathway to Somerhill Road which were donated by Mrs Flora Sassoon.

This stout rustic fence prevented children from falling into the pond. It also provided a romantic perch for the young lady in the enormous hat.

The council agreed to purchase a bandstand in 1912 costing £120 and manufactured by Macfarlane and Co. Before that bands had played under the temporary bandstand.

The Lodge House stood at the entrance to the gardens in Furze Hill and was constructed in the 1880s. Its predecessor had been a small thatched cottage. In 1912 Mrs Sassoon donated several items to furnish the Lodge including a stag's head, a pair of ibex antlers and two fox's heads.

In the background can be seen Grasshopper Cottage. In the foreground is the ship's figurehead given by Mrs Sassoon in 1913 to commemorate George V's accession. In 1908 Mrs Sassoon donated the clock which was fixed to the exterior of the Well House.

Mrs Flora Sassoon also purchased two plots of land near the Somerhill entrance and presented them to Hove Council who had not been able to afford them in 1907. The ground was made into croquet lawns and Mrs Sassoon added the Cumberland turf, two rustic summer houses, eight rustic chairs and two croquet sets. This view shows the official opening on 1 May 1913.

The entrance to the gardens from Somerhill Road was once graced with this statue, yet again presented by Mrs Sassoon in 1913. It is a draped figure of the goddess Polyhymnia, one of the nine Greek Muses.

A delightful view of the gardens taken in the late 1920s. It gives a close-up view of the decorative urns. The elevated clock on the right still stands.

THE GOLDSTONE & HOVE PARK

The Goldstone had excited people's curiosity for many years. In fact its popularity led to its downfall, literally. In the nineteenth century people would ride over from Brighton to visit the Goldstone and speculate as to whether it was a holy stone of the Druids or a sacrificial altar or merely an ordinary sarsen. It made William Marsh Rigden, who farmed the land, very cross indeed. He did not mind the interest but he did mind the way people left his gates open and trampled across the crops. So he had the Goldstone buried. The date of the deed is contested – some sources say 1833 or 1834 and others that it was 1845. But there is no dispute about the date it was unearthed again – 29 September 1900.

William Hollamby, one of the old Hove Commissioners, was the man who set about discovering where the Goldstone lay buried and he made sure it was brought to light and set up where the public could see it once more. The first name chosen for Hove Park was Goldstone Park and Alderman Henriques was very much in favour of it. But the idea was referred back to committee and eventually thrown out.

Ancient Stones Gouldstone Bottom (circa 1828)

An interesting fact about the Goldstone is that it could have been an outlier, that is a single, upright stone used as a foresight to a stone circle. There was a circle of stones arranged over an area of 100 yards north of the Goldstone. H.G. Hine drew this sketch in about 1828 and it shows sixteen stones, twelve of them forming the rough segment of a circle.

This drawing by R.H. Nibbs, on the other hand, is completely different. Only six stones are shown. The circle was destroyed in the 1840s. Some say the stones were broken up and used in the base of the Victoria Fountain in Brighton; others maintain that the stones were used to fill in a small pond at Goldstone and that later Hollamby unearthed them too.

The Goldstone unearthed, 29 September 1900. It seems curious that when the Goldstone was buried, only the names of two labourers, Churcher and Terry, have come down to us whereas in this photograph it obviously needed more than two to bring it to light.

The Goldstone in its new resting place in Hove Park, May 1906. Surrounding it are the stones which Hollamby rescued from the pond and believed to be some of the original ones.

By the 1920s, when this view was taken, the Goldstone and its satellites were neatly fenced in. It also shows another aspect of the Goldstone first recognized by prolific local artist Clem Lambert in 1913. Standing at the Old Shoreham Road and looking north he could discern a face in the rock, and he made a sketch to prove his point calling it Rockfeller.

Hove Park was opened on 24 May 1906 by the Mayor of Hove, Bruce Morison. Hove Council had agreed to purchase the 40 acres from the Stanford estate in 1899. The land cost £14,600 plus £400 for legal expenses. There was also the matter of compensation to the tune of £3,552 for the tenants who had been cultivating the land.

It was fortunate that the opening was blessed by splendid weather as about 3,000 children from Hove's public elementary schools attended. The girls wore white dresses with red sashes and rosettes of red, white and blue. In the left background a banner proclaims 'Portland Road Schools'.

Dancing round the maypole was the main tableau. The long procession, which started from Hove Town Hall at 2.30 p.m., included all the children, the dignitaries, mounted police, the RNVR with gun, the Hove Fire Brigade with steamer and the maypole girls walking behind the Bugle Band from Steyning Union Workhouse.

The great gale of 16/17 October 1987 had a disastrous effect on Hove Park which lost 450 mature trees. It is ironic that Hove should have been so successful in keeping Dutch elm disease under control only to have a great many healthy elms knocked out by a gale.

Tree surgeon Alan Greaves from Mevagissy received an unexpected windfall. He was clearing up the debris in Hove Park when he came across three dirty old mugs which turned out to be solid silver German seventeenth-century tankards. In August 1989 an inquest at Hove Town Hall decided they were treasure trove and, as the Crown did not want them, the coroner awarded them to Mr Greaves.

HOVE RECREATION GROUND & ALDRINGTON RECREATION GROUND

Hove Recreation Ground was Hove's first public open space. There was a desperate need for it, as can be gauged from a petition sent to the Hove Commissioners in 1887 signed by 1,726 Hove children hoping 'that you will favour us by opening the recreation ground before long. Our holidays are rapidly approaching and we have nowhere to play but in the streets . . . we cannot play cricket or football in the streets; if we play at marbles, either carts come along and break them or we are turned away'.

Although the 20 acres were purchased from the Stanford estate in 1887, the recreation ground was not officially opened until 2 May 1891. Alderman Howlett was insistent that it should be called a recreation ground as it was intended primarily for children, whereas a park implied a place for the pleasure of the wealthy classes who had plenty of other opportunities.

When Aldrington was annexed by Hove in 1893 one of the conditions was that Hove must purchase not less than 10 acres of land in Aldrington for a recreation ground. In fact 12 acres were bought in 1895, part of a field west of Wish Field.

This postcard shows the Hove Police smartly turned out to celebrate Empire Day, 1910, standing outside the gates of the recreation ground. Before the ground could be laid out Mr J.J. Clark had to be compensated for the loss of 12 acres of market garden and a footpath to West Blatchington had to be diverted.

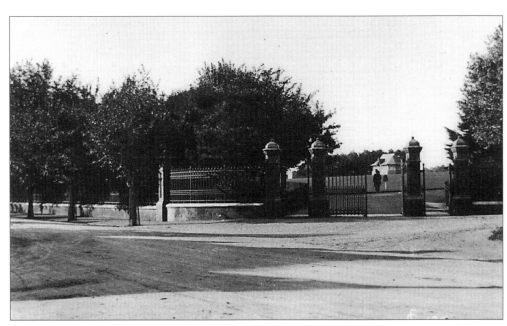

The gate piers and dwarf walls were constructed by Parsons and Sons, but the most expensive items were the cast iron gates and railings made by C.G. Reed and Son at a cost of £775. Not surprisingly the impressive entrance soon gave way to more humble fencing on either side.

The drinking fountain was donated by Alderman J.W. Howlett and was put up in 1893 by Parsons and Sons who charged £24 12s 3d for fixing the granite steps and laying on the water. In 1892 the borough surveyor, H.H. Scott, drew up plans for the fine looking pavilion, which was erected at a cost of £284.

The dell was laid out at the beginning. It was reached by a sloping path and, as the surrounding ground was higher, it provided a sheltered spot on a windy day.

Although this view was taken ten years after Aldrington Recreation Ground was opened, it is interesting to see that the land to the north was still mainly rural. The two houses on the corner of Portland Avenue were completely isolated.

A motor gymkhana at Aldrington Recreation Ground, 29 June 1910. It was organized by the Automobile Section of the Sussex Motor Yacht Club who had to assure Hove Council that steel-studded tyres would not be permitted.

FILM PIONEERS

The year 1996 sees celebrations for the centenary of the cinema, so it is only fitting that a section should be devoted to film pioneers; especially when two of them are recognized not just in the annals of local history, but are also of international importance. In the 1890s George Albert Smith and James Williamson began making their first films at Hove. There were no manuals to study, few people to approach for advice – they were working in a new field and of necessity they had to be innovative and persistent. Smith produced the first close-up, the first double exposure and the first commercially produced colour film. Williamson was fascinated with x-rays (called röntgen rays then) and he gave public exhibitions of them. He also produced a special effects camera so that film could run forwards or backwards, and he experimented with 'talkies'. These were only some of their achievements.

Their films were not what we mean by movies today. They were in fact optical illusions because the films were really still photographs shot at a rate of sixteen or twenty per second and then shown in rapid succession to create the idea of movement.

George Albert Smith leased St Ann's Well Gardens from 1892 and his film studio was based here from 1897 until 1903. This dramatic still comes from *The Little Witness* which he shot in the gardens.

All the early films were shot by natural light which is why the south coast was an ideal place. Film making ceased during the winter. This set, also at St Ann's Well, was used for *Mary Jane's Mishap*, the sad tale of a housemaid who cannot get the fire going and so resorts to paraffin with disastrous results.

Although George Albert Smith looks quite stern in this portrait, he enjoyed making comedies. In 1897 he produced thirty-one films, including *Making Sausages*. Doubtless the film today would go down like a lead balloon because it shows dogs and cats going into a machine at one end and emerging as sausages at the other. But his audience found it amusing.

James Williamson was Scottish by birth and, as he was born in 1855, he was certainly no youngster when he started to be fascinated by film making in the 1890s. He also had a wife and large family to support. He is seen here in the back row while his wife sits in front with their children clustered around.

Williamson earned his living as a chemist and his premises at 144 Church Road (now renumbered as 156) are seen here. In 1996 a special 'Cinema 100' plaque was unveiled here to commemorate his first film laboratory. Both he and Smith must have had considerable energy working away to the small hours on their films and inventions.

Williamson shot some of his films on location in Hove. One of his favoured spots was Ivy Lodge where Major and Mrs Vallance used to live until Brooker Hall was built. This photograph is taken from *Attack on a China Mission*. Another famous Williamson film shot at Ivy Lodge was *Fire!*

Williamson's film studios at Cambridge Grove, 1911. By this time he had sold his chemist's shop to devote himself to film making. But he was luckier than Smith because he got out of film making before the Americans swamped the market. Instead he moved to London where he and his sons built up a successful business making film apparatus.

Hove's first purpose-built cinema was erected in George Street and called variously the Electric Theatre or Hove Electric Empire. It was opened on 11 April 1911. In common with other cinemas built at around the same time, such as the Duke of York's at Brighton and the Prince's Imperial Picture Palace at Portslade, the façade was highly decorative.

An appreciative young audience outside the George Street cinema, 1923. Hove's cinemas laboured under a distinct disadvantage because Hove Council would not allow them to open on a Sunday, whereas the cinemas of Brighton, Portslade and Southwick were merrily cashing in on the sabbath. Although this cinema lasted until after the 'talkies', it could not hope to compete with the newer, larger cinemas and closed in 1934.

The cinema at Haddington Street was only a stone's throw from the one in George Street and was called the Empire Picture Theatre. Harry Scriven had it converted from an assembly hall and films were first shown here in 1910. His son, Eddie Scriven, was the projectionist. The manager, Robert Flint, used to drive around in an open top car with Eddie standing up to operate the large camera to record local happenings. Three days later the film would be shown. This photograph shows Eddie outside his cinema which closed in 1933.

THE OLD TOWN HALL

The building of Hove Town Hall was an expensive undertaking, but it was viewed as a tangible sign that Hove had arrived at last. There was already a town hall, but this was tucked away in the east part of town at Brunswick Street West and besides it had been built for the old Brunswick Town Commissioners. Now it was felt that something up to date and more centrally placed was essential. The architect chosen was Alfred Waterhouse and the town hall was built in bold red brick with terracotta dressings. The site was purchased in 1877 and James Warnes Howlett laid the foundation stone on 22 May 1880 and opened it on 13 December 1882. Howlett, who was known as the 'Father of Hove', was held in such high esteem that he was chosen for the honour rather than inviting a member of the royal family.

It was not so long ago that people who knew about architecture would scoff at Waterhouse's town hall as a frightful example of Victorian building. But now that the old town hall has gone and Victorian style is more admired, people look back with nostalgia.

Representatives of Hove Corporation and Boulogne Corporation, *c.* 1928. It is also an impressive portrait of the magnificent canopy outside the entrance to Hove Town Hall.

One of Hove Town Hall's most impressive features was the clock tower which also housed a carillon of twelve bells. The carillon could play fourteen tunes on two alternating barrels. On Mondays you would hear either 'Home, Sweet Home' or 'God Bless the Prince of Wales'. On special occasions the carillon could be disconnected and the bells played manually.

The Great Hall arranged for an industrial exhibition, September 1909. Not surprisingly the hall was in constant demand; it had been licensed for the performance of plays since 1889 and electricity was installed in 1894.

The Hove School of Music once gave lessons to Dame Clara Butt and so its twenty-first anniversary in 1925 was a special occasion. The hall has also been the venue for many lectures and John Cowper Powys gave his first one here. In January 1936 Grey Owl delivered one of his popular lectures.

A huge crowd gathered to hear George V proclaimed king, 9 May 1910. The mayor was Alderman Captain A.B.S. Fraser, who had been a captain in the 3rd Queen's Regiment. Note the large hanging lamp which is missing from the first photograph in this section.

In 1910 the mace bearer was Inspector William Fox who had served for twenty-three years in the Hove Police before being appointed to the post in 1900. As mace bearer he earned £5 5s 0d a year and he was given the uniform. The mace was presented to Hove Council in 1899 by Mortimer Singer.

This coat of arms used to adorn the wall above the west side of the entrance canopy. It has been preserved and set into a wall in the town hall piazza. Three black bugle horns are the arms of the Bellingham family who occupied Hangleton Manor in the sixteenth century.

The Hove coat of arms was also rescued from the old town hall. It is interesting to note that the saltire (the St Andrew's cross) also appears in the Abergavenny coat of arms and the Marquess of Abergavenny owned much of West Blatchington until the 1930s.

The town hall was burned down in the early hours of 9 January 1966. It was the most disastrous fire in Hove's history up until that date. Firefighters came from a wide area and there were seventy firemen using twelve pumps, three turntable ladders, two turntable ladders with fixed jets and twelve hand jets. Until 3.30 a.m. nobody knew there were six people trapped inside but the town hall keeper Stanley Burtenshaw, his wife, children and two friends were all rescued. The mace and mayor's regalia were rescued by John Barter, the mayor's secretary. It is ironic that Hove Council had taken steps to improve the fire precautions and had already set aside £7,000 towards it.

SHOPS & COMMERCE

Hove's first shopping scheme was a disaster. The idea was that a covered market should be built to serve the Brunswick area. So in 1826 the grandiose market house was erected by the architect Charles Augustin Busby. It did not open until 1828 and even though Busby offered to let stall-holders ply their trade rent free, the venture never took off. Soon it was turned into a riding school.

Meanwhile shops were appearing along Western Road and as Church Road was built up so the shops extended westwards until they joined up with those already existing in Cliftonville. Some of the premises had beautiful shop fronts with well proportioned windows and decorative iron work, while those connected with food were embellished with the best glazed tiles – not always white, but sometimes rich blue or brown, green and maroon. A few samples still survive.

No Victorian or Edwardian lady expected to carry her shopping home. There was a whole army of young men or boys with push-bikes or hand-carts to deliver the merchandise. Alternatively provision shops supplied their customers with leather bound order books, the name of the establishment gold-stamped on the cover. Ordered items would be delivered without the lady having to step outside her front door.

The Brighton Brewery was built in 1852 at the top of Osborne Villas and caused a huge obstruction commonly called the bunion. People began agitating for its removal in 1880 but the owner, Mr Weekes, never bothered to answer the council's letters.

The bunion from the west side. In 1900 Tamplins took over the brewery and are said to have requested £16,000 for the whole site. But Hove Council only wanted that portion which needed to be demolished for road widening. Eventually a deal was worked out and the brewery was demolished in 1902.

The block containing the Sackville Dining Rooms at 177 Church Road was built in the 1890s. From 1896 until 1906 the premises fulfilled the role of dining rooms, albeit with a different proprietor every year. Some of the beautiful ceramic tiles at the side remain to this day.

Charlie Ham's shop, 212 Church Road. Although it was an ironmongery shop, he also kept a substantial chicken run at the back in case his customers wanted a boiling fowl. The shop's interior was festooned with merchandise, each item priced in code so that Charlie could charge according to his customer's means.

George Street looks like a ghost town in this view taken in 1942 during an air raid alert. Behind the sandbags on the left is Broadley's shop, 'outfitters to men and boys', with a prominent advertisement for Swallow raincoats.

The all-clear has sounded and people are trying to resume their normal life. But normal life did not include parking in George Street as this was not allowed in the 1940s. To the right is the heavily protected frontage of Shaw's Stores, located there from 1862 to 1964.

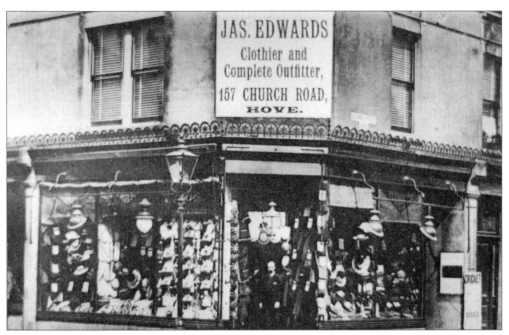

James Edwards ran this outfitter's and tailor's shop at 157 Church Road on the corner of George Street from the 1890s. By 1903 he was advertising himself as a hosier and boot warehouseman too. In 1923 Mr Broadley purchased the premises, but he did not change the name over the shop straight away.

This was the scene outside Broadley's on 16 June 1962 when the Queen and the Duke of Edinburgh walked down George Street, officially inaugurating the street after the improvement scheme had been completed. Practically every Hove policeman was on duty, all wearing immaculate white gloves.

The Royal George was built in George Street in the 1860s on a site once occupied by a small farmhouse. It was reconstructed in 1924 and demolished in 1965. The Attwater family were licensees for thirty-eight years and Doris Attwater married Jimmy Coe, brother of the well-known George Street fishmonger.

Martin Welch ran the Market House at 86 Westbourne Street from 1898 until 1907. This marvellous photograph dates from about 1907 and obviously shows a Christmas display with Christmas trees, evergreens and mistletoe.

The West Brighton Dispensary was founded in 1875 at 9 Church Road, West Brighton. The same premises are still occupied by a chemist, but it is now numbered as 105 Church Road. For many years it was known as Parris and Greening, two men who went into partnership in 1894. The original fitments remained in place until the 1980s and some have been preserved.

Robert Peel was Parris and Greening's qualified chemist from 1927 to 1977, becoming something of a local institution. In the early days he made all the preparations himself; there were five different sizes of pestle and mortar made of porcelain to use for crushing and mixing. Pills were handmade and often given a final coating of gold or silver leaf.

John Frowd took over Watson's dairy at 1 Alice Street in 1881 and by 1894 he had another premises at 88 Western Road on the corner of Lansdowne Place. Note the smartly turned out roundsmen and their

This magnificent shop front belonged to Henry Gilbey who ran his baker's shop at 40 Western Road, on the corner of Brunswick Street West, from 1892 to 1907, when it was taken over by Gigins. In the background the Freemason's Tavern can be seen.

The Wick Motor Garage in Davigdor Road was near the Hove Electric Light Works; it was the sole district agent for Daimler cars. In 1907 an advertisement stated that 'all work is carried out under the personal supervision of Mr R.W.R. Gill, the proprietor, a gentleman of much up-to-date skill, and who has carefully studied both the theoretical and mechanical construction of vehicles'.

William Balchin and Sons ran quite a large business as florists and seedsmen. This shop was situated at 160–162 Church Road (on the corner of St Aubyns) and there was another one at 87 Western Road, Brighton. They had extensive nurseries in the Upper Drive.

Hills of Hove was established in 1898. In its heyday so many people wanted to work there that they kept a waiting list of hopeful applicants. The staff had to be smartly dressed with perhaps some discreet jewellery, but no cardigan was allowed. So refined was the image that in later days, when an elderly lady spotted a bikini in the window she threatened to call the police. The store closed in 1982.

This grandiose building hardly resembles the popular notion of a local co-op but in fact the Palmeira Stores were run by the Brighton and Hove Co-operative Supply Association from the 1870s. The building was erected in the 1860s as the Palmeira Hotel but somehow the scheme fell through and it was still unoccupied in 1866.

IRONMONGERY, GAS, AND ELECTRIC LIGHT FITTINGS DEPARTMENT.

SECOND FLOOR.

ELECTRIC LIGHT FITTINGS.

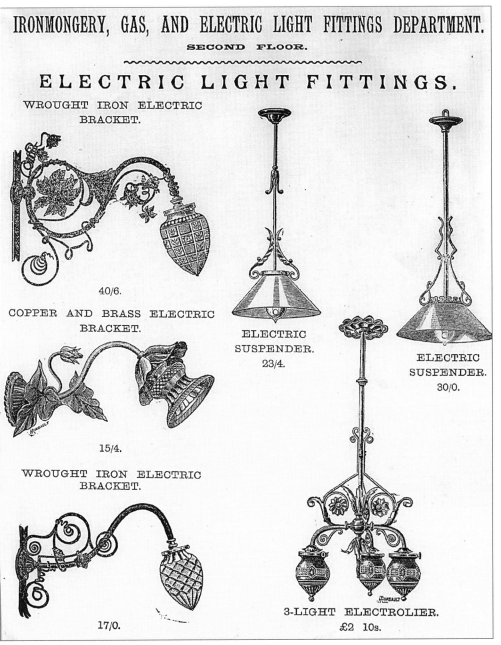

WROUGHT IRON ELECTRIC BRACKET.

40/6.

COPPER AND BRASS ELECTRIC BRACKET.

15/4.

WROUGHT IRON ELECTRIC BRACKET.

17/0.

ELECTRIC SUSPENDER.

23/4.

ELECTRIC SUSPENDER.

30/0.

3-LIGHT ELECTROLIER.

£2 10s.

Palmeira Stores was the ultimate department store — you could buy virtually anything under its roof. For instance in 1891 in the poultry department you could purchase pheasants, partridges, black game, widgeon, wood pigeon, bourdeaux pigeon besides wild duck and geese. There were Oriental carpets, mandolins and guitars, lobsters and oysters, jewelled lamps and electrical fittings, expensive furs, champagne (1880 and 1884 vintage), not to mention saddles and harnesses for your horse.

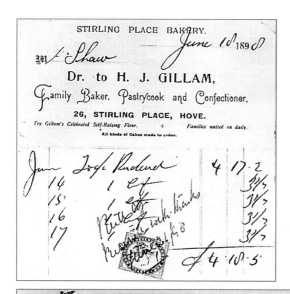

Mr Gillam ran a bakery in Stirling Place from 1882 to 1911. From the invoice it appears that Mr Gillam produced his own flour and that families were 'waited on daily'.

A receipt dating from 1919 from Hove Borough Council reveals that more money was collected for the poor rate than for the district rate. The item at the end, for private enclosures only, applied to people living in the Brunswick and Adelaide area who had to pay for the upkeep of the communal gardens.

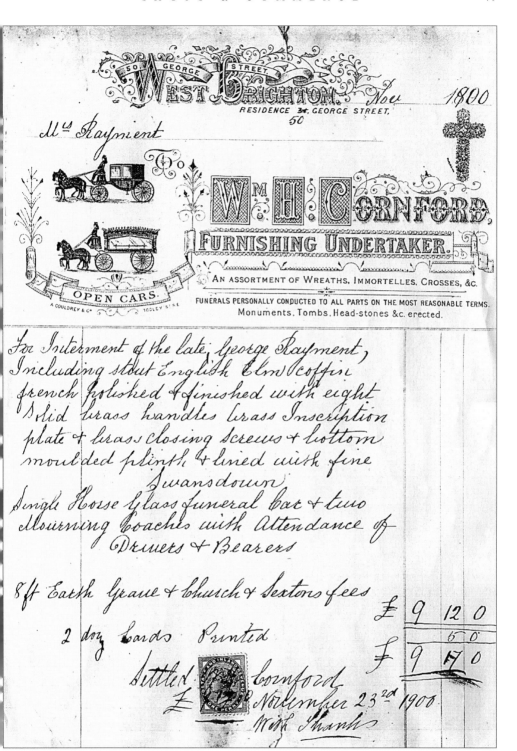

For Interment of the late George Rayment, Including stout English Elm coffin french polished & finished with eight Solid brass handles brass Inscription plate & brass closing screws & bottom moulded plinth & lined with fine Swansdown Single Horse Glass funeral Car & two Mourning Coaches with Attendance of Drivers & Bearers

8 ft Earth Grave & Church & Sextons fees £ 9 12 0

2 doz Cards Printed 5 0

£ 9 7 0

Settled Cornford November 23rd 1900 With Thanks

Cornford's the undertaker was a long established business at 50 George Street, starting out in the 1890s and remaining until the 1980s when it moved. The illustration at the top of the bill shows an elaborate glass funeral coach of the type used for Canon Peacey.

Mr Shaw   June 16   1896

Dr. to

F. WRIGHT,
UPHOLSTERER, CABINET MAKER,
BEDDING MANUFACTURER,
AND
GENERAL HOUSE FURNISHER,
85 & 87, BLATCHINGTON RD., WEST BRIGHTON

Iron Bedsteads, Fenders, Fireirons. Floor Cloth, Carpets, Hearth
Rugs, Matting, &c.
ALL KINDS OF FURNITURE LET ON HIRE.
Furniture Re-stuffed, Covered and Polished to Equal New.
Carpets Taken up, Beaten and Re-laid.

Balance of A/c Enclosed   £   4 . 11 . ?

June 20/98

F. Wright, cabinet-maker, started his business at 87 Blatchington Road in 1880 and by 1896 he had expanded into the adjacent shop. The business was still going strong in the 1960s. It is interesting to note that in 1878 Blatchington Road housed 428 inhabitants.

J. Chapman started his Rising Sun Laundry at 1 Arthur Street in 1904. The laundry was done on the premises and there was a large open drying ground at the back. He also undertook carpet beating by machine and in another building he operated a glove cleaning business.

The gymnasium in Holland Road, erected in 1883 and run by Charles Hutton Moss. In 1896, while the Duke and Duchess of York were staying with Mr and Mrs Reuben Sassoon at Hove, the whole party turned up at the gymnasium to watch an exhibition of fancy cycle riding by lady riders. In 1928 the building was sold and converted into a synagogue.

The coast road before it was called Kingsway, *c.* 1905. The woman on the left with apron and basket is a flower seller who made a precarious living selling flowers or buttonholes. She was also to be seen near the little goat carriages.

The road in front of Palmeira Mansions, which once had a hackney carriage stand, *c.* 1906. The year 1892 was a terrible one for cab owners – there were too many of them trying to scratch a living, the cost of corn and hay was high and there was an epidemic of influenza among visitors as well as among cab horses.

THE VALLANCE FAMILY

The Vallance family moved to Hove from Patcham in the 1780s. John Vallance (*c.* 1732–1794) was the elder son of James and Esther Vallance who had caused such a commotion by eloping, a matter not improved by Esther's father being rector of Southwick. John Vallance married Deborah Mighel at Brighton in 1756 and they had five children. It is generally stated that John Vallance built Hove Manor House in about 1785, but what seems more probable is that he modernized the house already there, which had also been remodelled prior to 1750. The south-east front was faced with knapped flint, while the south-west façade was designed in the late Georgian manner and covered with what was called Roman cement. In this house the Prince Regent is reputed to have stayed as a guest of John Vallance's son, also called John, whom he met at a cricket match.

The original John Vallance had a grandson called Benjamin Vallance who became the first house surgeon of the Royal Sussex County Hospital. Benjamin's brother, another John Vallance, was an inventor whose most famous patent was no. 4905, taken out in 1824; it was the first patent for working a railway by means of atmospheric pressure. However, he was ahead of his time and he died suddenly in modest lodgings in Western Road, Hove.

This portrait and the following three are still to be seen at Hove Museum. However, they are only a small selection of what must have been an extensive series of family portraits which John Olliver Vallance was desperate to keep together. After his death they seem to have been dispersed to various branches of the family. James Vallance (1766–1847), seen here, was the grandson of James and Esther Vallance and the uncle of John Brooker Vallance. (see p. 75)

James Vallance married Ann Catt at Lewes, 17 November 1790. It is probable that she was connected with the Catt family who later leased Bishopstone tidemills. In the 1820s a William Catt became associated with the Vallance Brewery at West Street, Brighton and for many years the firm of Vallance and Catt was well known in the area. At one time the firm owned the Ship Inn in Hove Street. This portrait of Ann, and the companion one of her husband (opposite), were painted in about 1840.

John Brooker Vallance (1804–1851) was the grandson of John Vallance who rebuilt Hove Manor. The name Brooker came from his mother's maiden name. John Brooker was greatly interested in hare coursing and founded the Brighton harriers who used to wear a dark-green hunting jacket. It may be that he chose this outfit when he sat for his portrait. In spite of his healthy looks and outdoor life he died aged forty-seven on Christmas Day – the same day his infant brother had died in 1802.

The portrait of John Brooker and this one of his wife Sarah Duke Olliver Vallance were painted in about 1850. She survived her husband for another thirty-nine years. A tablet in St Andrew's Church was erected by her 'as a tribute of affectionate regard to one who was a kind husband, a tender father and a sincere friend'. She was left with two small sons, the younger of whom died nine years later leaving John Olliver Vallance to receive her undivided attention.

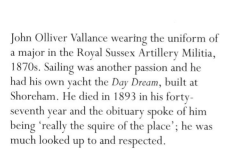

Sarah Vallance, *c.* 1870. There seems to have been some tension between her and John Olliver when he decided to marry the daughter of a local schoolmaster at the age of twenty. It was a very quiet wedding and there was no junketing for the tenants of the Vallance estate.

John Olliver Vallance wearing the uniform of a major in the Royal Sussex Artillery Militia, 1870s. Sailing was another passion and he had his own yacht the *Day Dream*, built at Shoreham. He died in 1893 in his forty-seventh year and the obituary spoke of him being 'really the squire of the place'; he was much looked up to and respected.

The Vallance family's home was actually called Hove House until 1867 when John Olliver bought the manorial rights. Except for a couple of years in the 1900s, the Vallances ceased to live at Hove Manor after old Mrs Vallance died in 1890. It was demolished in the 1930s.

After John Olliver married Emma Kate they went to live at Ivy Lodge, a house not far from Hove Manor. It was not until 1877 that Major Vallance had Brooker Hall constructed to the designs of Thomas Lainson. Although Emma had produced no children in the ten years at Ivy Lodge, not long after moving to their new home her first son was born, to be followed by two more sons and two daughters.

Vane de Valence Mortimer Vallance (1885–1924) was the son of Edward Vallance, who lived for many years in a large house in St Aubyns. He was descended from the James Vallance who married Ann Catt (see pp. 76–7). Vane joined the 5th Lancers straight from Sandhurst and although he saw continuous action during the First World War, serving through the retreat from Mons and at both Battles of Ypres, he survived unscathed. He was awarded the Military Cross and by the time he went to serve in India he held the rank of major. It is ironic that such a hardened soldier should have met his death back home by walking too near the edge of the cliffs at Black Rock and falling over. Suicide was discounted. He was thirty-nine years old and his only child, a daughter called Vivien, was about five.

SCHOOLS

Right from the early days Hove was well known for its private schools. Hove College claimed to be the earliest, dating from 1796, while not far away was Dr Morell's Academy where I.K. Brunel was a pupil in 1820. At 32 Brunswick Terrace in the 1830s there was a very exclusive school for young ladies where the social graces were imparted at a considerable expense to their papas – it cost at least £1,000 for two years. Many of the schools were tiny establishments which came and went with alarming frequency. Some schools advertised for 'colonial' pupils, that is children sent back home for education while their parents were busy abroad. In the Brunswick area along there were thirty-eight private schools in 1871. By 1930 the numbers for the whole of Hove had dwindled to seven boys' schools and nine girls' schools.

By comparison state education made a slow start. At Hove the earliest schools (at Farman Street, Ivy Place and George Street) were founded at the instigation of local vicars rather than by government decree. In spite of the fact that parents had to pay a few pence for their children's education, the schools were crammed to capacity and coping with the numbers was a perennial problem.

Ivy Place School, 2 November 1914; note that the girls have been knitting. Education for the poor in this part of Hove came at the instigation of the Revd Thomas Rooper and for six years he paid for it out of his own pocket. In 1840 enough money was raised by subscription to build a school in Farman Street. Miss Rooper founded the school in Ivy Place in the 1840s.

St Andrew's School was another school run under the auspices of the Church of England. It was the Revd Walter Kelly, vicar of Hove, who started things moving and the school was erected in 1858 and enlarged in 1870 and again in 1894. Originally known as the George Street Schools or the West Hove National Schools, by 1961 a new name was chosen, St Andrew's School.

The Ellen Street Schools were built to accommodate 800 children and were opened in 1879. In 1909 about thirty of the children were found to be suffering from malnutrition. In 1958 it was renamed Goldstone School and, after a long campaign for new premises, the building was closed in 1974 and demolished.

The Connaught Road Schools opened in 1884 and this photograph of pupils dates from the 1880s. Demand was high and by 1904 the average attendance was put at 736, although officially there was only enough space for 706. In 1904 His Majesty's Inspector commented that discipline in the infants' school was very good and the instruction quite satisfactory.

Aldrington National Schools were built in 1888 and were run as Church of England Schools until 1903 when Hove Education Committee took charge. Poor pupils were issued with vouchers for free boots – better off ones joined the school boot club and saved 3*d* a week. This photograph dates from 1909 and the teacher on the left is Miss Johnson.

Hove County School for Boys, formally opened on 28 October 1936 when, among others, Earl de la Warr, the Bishop of Chichester and the Mayor of Hove were present. It cost £45,000 and only two years previously the land was still cultivated farmland, part of West Blatchington Court Farm which can be seen in the background with the windmill on the left.

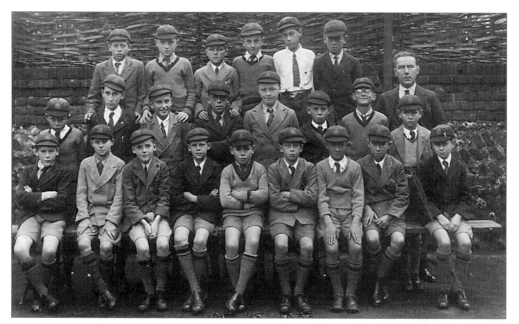

The 4th form at Hove High School with their teacher, Samuel Watson, *c.* 1933. The school was situated at 49 Clarendon Villas from 1884 to 1959. A plaque put up for the twenty-seven old boys killed in the First World War is still in place by the entrance. Captain A.B. Wales, later Mayor of Hove, was an old boy and so was Peter Jackson who ran an illustrated series called 'Strange Facts of London' in the *Evening Standard*.

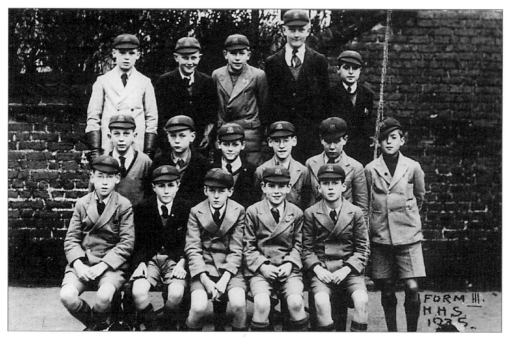

The 3rd form at Hove High School, 1935. In the front row, second from the left, is John Broomfield whose father owned a good deal of farmland in Portslade. The headmaster from 1931 until 1951 was the Revd Jack Kingston, vicar of St Mary's, Brighton, and chaplain to Bishop Bell who often looked in on the school. Mr Kingston's favourite dictum was 'Smut, won't 'ave it'.

This school was originally known as Cliff House School, a name which can be seen at the top of the building. Underneath are the words Hove College, which it became in 1894. To the right can be seen old buildings in Hove Street. The school stayed at this location until 1935, when it moved a short way along Kingsway to Langton House.

Hove College's football team, 1934. On the left in splendid plus-fours can be seen R.L.C. Jackson, headmaster, and on the right is his dog Peter. The first XI played fourteen matches, won thirteen and drew one.

A photograph of the hallway in Langton House after it became Hove College. On the right of the door is a panel listing past headmasters. During the Second World War the building was requisitioned and the school had to move to Wedmore in Somerset.

Hove College's library was located in the former billiard room. As can be seen, it boasted a splendid fireplace. There was another good fireplace in the dining room which also had panelling on the walls.

Mowden School takes its name from Mowden Hall, Hatfield Peverel in Essex where it was founded in 1896. The school was at Lansdowne Place, Hove, from 1901 to 1913 before it moved to new premises in The Droveway where this photograph was taken shortly afterwards. The school looks much the same today except for the addition of 15 ft to the east end and a large quantity of ivy.

Mowden School is a family run business. Started by B.A. Snell and A.P. Snell, it passed to Edward Snell in 1937 and Christopher Snell, grandson of the founder, took over in 1973. Sisters, aunts and wives have all played their part in running the school. The Snell family are seen gathered around their car outside Mowden, 1913.

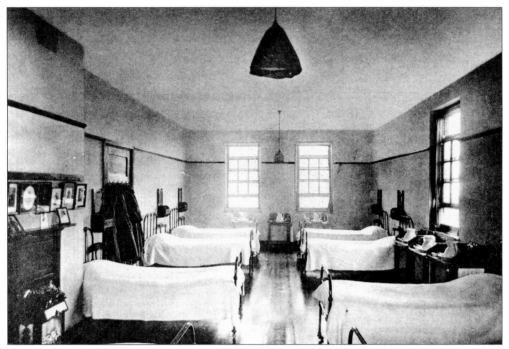

Mowden named all its rooms. Thus the four original form rooms were called Gordon, Livingstone, Lawrence and Wellington. This dormitory was called India.

The Mowden boys are seen here taking part in a little civilized gardening. But when the grounds were purchased it was either rough grass or ploughed land, while the soccer ground (bought in 1921) was so full of stones that the boys used to pick up 100 each day.

St Christopher's is also a family run school. It began in Sackville Road in 1927, moved to 56 New Church Road and finally to 33 New Church Road (its present location) in 1944. In 1947 Maurice Saunders began teaching there and he was headmaster from 1956 to 1978; then his son Roger took over. When they were both at the school they were known as 'Old Sir' and 'Young Sir'. This photograph was taken in 1981 and Mike Carter is the teacher.

This group of scholarship boys stands outside the entrance to St Christopher's with its attractive porch, 1960. The boys, left to right: P.L. Near, M.P.M. Nimmo, B.R. Dean, R.H. Baker, M.Q. Rose, R.W. Bidwell, J.A. Scott and N.L. Banks.

St Christopher's sports day was held in the school playing field at Glebe Villas. In the 1950s when this photograph was taken a smart display of drill was a highlight. Mr Saunders would lead the boys on to the field and they would all sing a good marching song such as 'Men of Harlech' or 'Sussex by the Sea'.

The PNEU School, 174 New Church Road, c. 1935. There were about forty pupils, but the school only lasted for a few years. Two of the girls had famous grandfathers – one was Anne Baden-Powell, granddaughter of Lord Baden-Powell, founder of the boy scout movement; the other was Anthea Gordon, granddaughter of General Gordon of Khartoum.

Hove's most famous schoolboy spent four years at the Misses Thomson's Preparatory School at 29 and 30 Brunswick Road. Red-haired Winston Churchill arrived here aged eight with a reputation of being a naughty child. But he enjoyed his time at Hove.

This privately erected plaque replaces an earlier stone one put up in 1953. Churchill actually attended the school from 1884 to 1888. His favourite subjects were English and History and he enjoyed learning reams of poetry. He also learned how to ride a horse.

CHURCHES

uilding new churches was practically a national pastime in Victorian England and especially so at Hove. They rebuilt the ancient churches and set about raising funds to erect new ones. But even in those days fund raising at Hove was a daunting task. Canon Peacey, talking about the difficulty of raising enough to build St Barnabas's Church, ascribed it to the large number of people who retired here from the colonies and wanted peace and quiet. Likewise there were people who thought it a waste of money to rebuild St Andrew's Church because there were so few living in the vicinity at that time. St Patrick's Church, which has such a fine interior, was built from private funds. But several new churches were built and St John's even acquired the spire designated in its plans while All Saints' had to make do with a stump of a tower.

The Victorians never envisaged the dramatic drop in church attendance. To put it baldly, Hove has too many churches. Some, like St Andrew's, Waterloo Street, have closed for good, while others have been converted to different uses – St Agnes's became a gym, the Methodist Church in Old Shoreham Road became home to the Grace Eyre Foundation, the redundant St Thomas's was sold to the Coptic Church while St Cuthbert's was demolished.

From this old print it is clear to see that St Andrew's Church was just a remnant of its former self. The arches of a larger building have been bricked up to provide a small chapel. The tower collapsed long ago in the sixteenth century. It is said that surplus stone was carted off to build a folly in Goodwood Park.

When the architect George Basevi restored St Andrew's he tried to use as much of the old material as possible. But the bell turret and the porch were taken down and the church was rebuilt to its original dimensions. It reopened on 18 June 1836. In this view the old iron gates are still in use and the lych-gate has not yet been built.

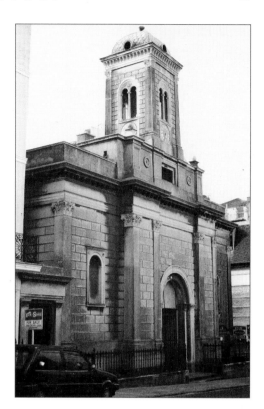

St Andrew's Church, Waterloo Street was built in 1827–8 by Charles Barry to cater for the fashionable throng who frequented Brunswick Town. Charles Augustin Busby, the architect of Brunswick Town, was disappointed not to be commissioned to design the church himself, but unfortunately he had already had a row with the Revd Edward Everard who owned the site.

The interior of St Andrew's, Waterloo Street. This chancel was not part of Barry's original plan but was created by his son in 1882 when the chapel was enlarged. Before that the altar had been plain; in 1874 the only ornament was the Holy Communion plate and the wall behind the altar had a painting of a plain black cross rising from a lurid red background.

St Peter's Church, West Blatchington, has the distinction of being the oldest church in Hove. It used to be thought that it was a twelfth-century Norman church, but recent archaeological investigations carried out by John Holmes have revealed Saxon work and therefore the original church must have been constructed in the eleventh century.

The church of St Helen stood in a fairly bleak spot far out in the countryside. Because the population was sparse and there were no ambitious plans for it, it has retained its medieval look to this day. But the church was in danger of crumbling away completely until Sir George Cokayne paid for the chancel and the tower to be repaired in 1870.

St. Leonard's Church, Aldrington.

In this view St Leonard's Church looks deceptively modern but it stands on an ancient site. From a high spot in the fourteenth century Aldrington suffered progressive decline until by the nineteenth century the church was a heap of rubble and nobody lived in the parish except the toll-gate keeper. The Ingram family restored the church in 1878. The first extension was finished in 1931, the second five years later.

The first meeting to consider building St Barnabas's was held in 1881. It was recognized as a necessity because of 'the large and increasing population in the north west . . . composed almost entirely of labouring people'. The architect, J.L. Pearson, produced what he called 'one of my cheap editions' and St Barnabas was consecrated in 1883.

St Patrick's Church, Cambridge Road, was opened in 1858. The architect was Henry Edward Kendall and, as can be seen from the print, he intended a lofty tower to occupy the north part of the site. The building was paid for by the Revd James O'Brien who became the first incumbent.

This print shows St Patrick's as it was actually built. People were enthusiastic about the entrance at the south end which meant you entered the church from a cloister rather than straight off the street. It became a fashionable church noted for the quality of its music.

The interior of St Patrick's has many lovely features. The height is impressive too – 70 ft from floor to roof. The beautiful frescoes seen here were designed by Clayton and Bell and finished in 1891. The saints are depicted in formal pose with canopies above their heads and the central part of the design, Christ in majesty, is painted high above the altar. The angels carved from wood above the frescoes were there right from the start. In order to preserve the frescoes from discolouration the church was converted from gas to electric lighting.

The Church of St Philip was consecrated in 1898. The exterior is polychrome at its most extraordinary for you will find Bath stone alternating with red brick, dark grey limestone and knapped flints, all in cheerful juxtaposition.

St Philip's was extended in 1909–10 on the west side and included a length of nave, three bays of the aisle, a baptistry and a porch. The two parts of the exterior have been cleverly matched and the only give-away is in the roof slates.

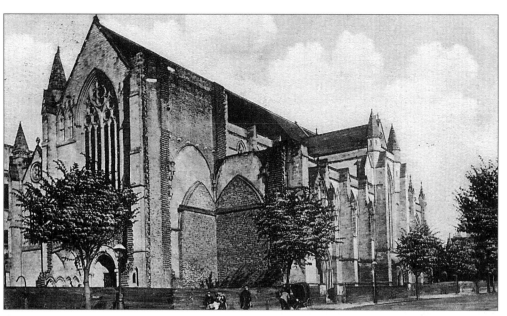

The first meeting to consider the building of All Saints' took place in 1886, but it was not until 1891 that the nave and aisles were consecrated. This view shows the raw place where the tower was going to be built, but by 1924 only the base had been completed.

All Saints' from the east, where it takes on almost cathedral-like proportions; the architect who created it, J.L. Pearson, also designed Truro Cathedral. By 1891 the church had already cost over £19,000 and that was before the choir and sanctuary, the organ and organ case, and the reredos had been added.

The beautiful interior of the Church of the Sacred Heart, Norton Road. In 1887 the Requiem Mass for Prince John of Bourbon was held here. His brother was Charles VI, known as the Count de Montemolin, pretender to the Spanish throne. Seven priests assisted at the mass and at either side of the catafalque stood three enormous yellow candles rising 10 ft from the nave.

Rutland Hall was built in 1900 and started out as a mission hall, the responsibility of the Congregational church in Ventnor Villas. During the First World War it was taken over by the military and afterwards it was sold and the money put towards the building of the Hounsom Memorial Church in Holmes Avenue.

The building housing the Seventh Day Adventist Church in Hove Place started life as a coach house to nearby Leicester Lodge. The Adventists used to meet in a room over a shop in Church Road until moving here in the 1930s. The denomination was founded in 1831 in the USA.

This postcard was produced to commemorate the death of General Booth (founder of the Salvation Army) in 1912, and his last visit to Hove in 1910. He was not the only famous preacher visiting Hove at that time – there was also the Revd Charles Spurgeon leading an eight-day mission at the Holland Road Baptist Church and Father Vaughan packing them in at the Sacred Heart.

Canon Peacey was a man of considerable importance at Hove, having been its vicar for almost thirty years. He admitted that he came to Hove with no light heart because he understood that the workload would be heavy. During his time he oversaw the expansion of the George Street Schools, the building of St Barnabas's Church and Vicarage and the building of All Saints' Church and Vicarage. He was married with three sons and seven daughters, but his two year old son died in 1891 and his wife died in 1899. Canon Peacey died on 1 April 1909 and was given a tremendous send-off. Even the King sent a message of sympathy.

BUILDINGS

The following pages reveal the variety of buildings to be seen at Hove. They range from the agricultural to grand town houses, from Regency terraces to an exotic Indian gateway and from a convent to a gentleman's club. It is amusing to recall the Revd W.H. Horsfield's disparaging description of Hove in the early nineteenth century as a 'mean and insignificant assemblage of huts'. He was no admirer of small flint cottages.

However, when building started on Brunswick Town it was on a grand scale. Although there are some architectural variations between the houses, the overall impression is one of uniformity. It could not be more different from the next major development – the Cliftonville area – where there was no ambitious plan and the houses were built piecemeal to individual tastes.

The West Brighton estate fell somewhere between the two. Although it started off in a similar way to Brunswick with grand terraces facing the sea (Queen's Gardens) it soon became apparent that people no longer wished to live in terraces, but in houses. Taste in colour also changed and whereas the first part of the West Brighton estate were built in white brick, later houses were constructed of red brick with plenty of embellishments.

Work on building Brunswick Terrace started in 1824. The Brunswick Square Act of 1830 stipulates that all front elevations must be maintained unaltered. Owners must also see that their houses are painted every five years.

Brunswick Square seen from the gardens. Note the iron railings which enclosed the gardens and lasted until the Second World War when they were removed for scrap. It is only recently that they have been replaced.

The unique sight of 42 and 43 Medina Villas. Built in the 1850s they have Dutch gables, curious chimneys sitting on their own brick plinths, little attic windows set in the slate roof and a diaper pattern in the red bricks composed of slate blue bricks.

In 1899 J.T. Chappell applied to build four brick villas between Grand Avenue and Third Avenue. This was one of them. Chappell was something of an expert in red brick because he also built Hove Town Hall and Hove Hospital, all embellished with terracotta.

This balcony is situated in Salisbury Road. However, it belongs to 33 Palmeira Mansions, which has a beautiful interior modelled in the 1880s to the instructions of Mr A.W. Mason, who was reputed to have made a fortune out of ink.

This delightfully rural view of West Blatchington Windmill was taken shortly after the fire of 3 May 1936 which destroyed the barn on the south side. Fortunately the wind was blowing from the north east otherwise the windmill would have been lost too.

The Jaipur Gateway in its original setting as the grand entrance to the Arts-Ware Court of the Indo-Colonial Exhibition at London, 1886. It was made in India as a gift for the Queen Empress.

Not long after Brooker Hall was turned into Hove Museum, the Jaipur Gateway was re-erected in its grounds. The Baroda Pigeon House on the left also came from the same exhibition, but was removed in 1959.

The railway bridge at Sackville Road was constructed in 1840 over what was then a country lane. Some sixty years later it had become totally inadequate for the amount of traffic using it and because of the brick buttresses people could not see what was coming beyond the arch. A survey taken on 28 August 1911 showed that 634 horse-drawn vehicles, 600 cycles, 215 hand barrows and 70 motors passed under the bridge on that day. Reconstruction was delayed by wrangling over cost-sharing between the railway company and Hove Council, but the bridge was finally replaced in 1927.

These four beautiful homes, called The Lawns, were built in 1904. They were the ultimate in luxurious living and not cheap either, costing between £7,000 and £8,000 each. For that price there was central heating, an 'electric Turkish bath', an electric lift and on the upper floors there were eight bedrooms and a library. As a final touch of opulence the domes were gilded.

In 1899 81 The Drive was built for Dr C.E. Whitcher. The billiard room and morning room were on the ground floor, while the consulting room, library and drawing room were on the first floor. The building was demolished in 1988.

The morning room of 81 The Drive faced west and overlooked the garden with a double set of french windows. Practically the whole of the south wall was taken up with the elaborate fireplace. This included two stained glass windows on either side, and above them to the side two paintings in alcoves, one of which is seen here.

Hove Club, *c.* 1908. Hove Club was erected in the 1890s. It looks much the same today, except that those extraordinary appendages on the chimneys have gone.

Hove Club was a gentlemen's club which had its fair share of military top brass in 1897, including ten major-generals and fifteen colonels. A gentleman could not just roll up and join; he had to be proposed and seconded and then the members would vote using this box. If they considered him undesirable he was blackballed.

The two houses seen here were all that remained of a group called Providence Place, built in the late 1840s. There was also a Providence Place at Brighton so to avoid confusion the Hove one was changed to Connaught Place in 1899. By 1916 this too had gone and the houses (next door to the library) were numbered as 178 and 180 Church Road. They were demolished in about 1961.

Hove Hospital was not called that until 1918. It was opened in 1888. Although the Chairman of the Hove Commissioners, Mr J.W. Howlett, gave £1,000 to endow the beds, it was three wealthy Hove ladies who came up trumps by donating an astonishing £8,750 between them.

St Joseph's Home was built in the 1880s and was run by the Little Sisters of the Poor, the first order to specialize in the care of the elderly. In 1954 there were eighteen nuns and 120 residents of both sexes and all creeds. By 1988 there were twelve nuns and forty-three residents. Then Sainsbury's purchased the site.

St Joseph's Home faced south and when it was built the Old Shoreham Road was little more than a track. The nuns had their own little cemetery, but after the purchase by Sainsbury's the company arranged for sixteen bodies to be removed in June 1988. The loss of trees and garden, to make way for the Homebase store, was much regretted by the neighbours.

Oonagh and Moyra Corcasden and their friend Joan Welby. The girls are playing on land where in the 1930s the millionaire Stuart Millar had his impressive grey-brick mansion built. It was known originally as 1 Princes Crescent, then as 157 Kingsway.

The plans for the Convalescent Police Seaside Home were approved in June 1892 and the building was finished a year later. At that time the road was called Bertram Road (now Portland Road). The home was the first of its kind and it was not uncommon for an officer to be sent there after being injured trying to stop a runaway horse.

MEMORIALS & EVENTS

Hove celebrated Empire Day with fervour. It was the day chosen for great events such as the opening of Aldrington Recreation Ground, Hove Park and St Ann's Well Gardens. The Empire was not a myth but a reality for many former Empire-builders who retired to Hove. There was a particularly strong link with India, hence the siting of the Jaipur Gateway here. Memorial stones record the wide range of their service – Assam, Benares, Bengal, Bombay, Calcutta, Ceylon, Darjeeling and Madras. Several residents were members of the elite Honourable East India Company's Service, of whom Sir George Dallas was one. While some served with exotic Indian regiments such as the Bengal Lancers or Rattray's Sikhs, others helped to build the railway system. Meanwhile Sir George Everest was busily engaged on the great trigonometrical survey of India of which he was appointed superintendent in 1823. Mount Everest was named after him. A shot of his tombstone in St Andrew's Churchyard appeared in the opening sequence of *The Conquest of Everest*, made in 1953. It had taken the film makers about six months to track down his last resting place at Hove.

This beautiful memorial to Sir George Dallas (1758–1833) was sculpted by Ternouth and is found at St Andrew's Church, Waterloo Street. Sir George served in Bengal and 'with attainments rare and elegant he united great abilities'. The Dallas clan came from the region of Elgin and Nairn in Scotland, but many left for the United States after the disastrous battle at Culloden.

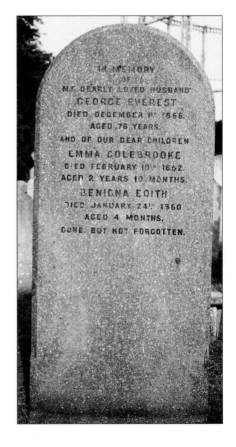

Sir George Everest (1709–1866) returning home from long service abroad did not marry until he was fifty-six years old. He was older than his father-in-law, Thomas Wing, who lies buried in the next plot. Sadly both Everest's daughters died young.

Admiral Sir George Augustus Westphal (1785–1875) is also buried in St Andrew's Churchyard. He led an eventful life seeing service in over 100 actions but returned home to live quietly at 2 Brunswick Square for thirty-nine years. When he died he was the last surviving officer of the Battle of Trafalgar (1805), where he had served aboard HMS *Victory*. His wounds were tended in the same cockpit where Nelson lay dying.

Martin Leonard Landfried (1834–1902) is buried in Hove Cemetery. He was a celebrated Hove resident and at his death was given an elaborate military funeral complete with gun carriage and muffled drums. He served in the 17th Lancers at the Battle of Balaclava, 25 October 1854, and was one of the men who sounded the charge. During the battle a bullet passed through his right arm, glanced off the pouch he wore at his side and killed his horse.

Amy Sedgwick (1830–97) was a famous
Victorian actress. When she retired to Hove
she performed a popular double act with
Martin Landfried, who sounded the bugle call
as he had at the charge of the Light Brigade
while Amy recited Tennyson's poem of the
same title. There was not a dry eye in the
house.

Ida Lupino (1918–95) spent about four years
at Clarence House School in Norman Road.
She went on to star in Hollywood films, but
later made her mark as a director, writer and
producer of films.

Alderman James Warnes Howlett attends the drumhead service held at Hove Recreation Ground, 1910. He died the following year. He kept a fine cellar and even in old age could offer his guests a choice of over fifty different wines.

The Lady Chichester Hospital was founded in 1905 and moved to New Church Road in 1920. A major fund raising event was the summer fête when a famous person would attend. In 1935 it was film star Frances Day, in 1945 it was Arthur Askey and in this photograph, taken in about 1947, it was the actress Evelyn Laye. At the back are boys from St Christopher's School.

Mr Bernard Baron was given exclusive use of St Ann's Well Gardens on 21 July 1915 so that he could give a party for wounded officers and soldiers. On arrival the men were presented with tobacco, cigarettes and chocolates, but the council had ruled that no intoxicants should be served.

During the First World War Hove collected £289,620 in National War Bonds and Savings Certificates. As an acknowledgement Hove was awarded its own tank which arrived in Hove Park on 23 September 1919. It was called 'Hova' and had seen action at Messines, Arras, Ypres and Cambrai. It survived until 1937 and then it was broken up for scrap metal.

Hove Town Hall was the venue for an exhibition by the Hove Camera Club founded in 1896. Two of their most important members were George Albert Smith and James Williamson. On 25 and 26 November 1897, at their second exhibition, Williamson demonstrated his röntgen rays and moving pictures were shown for the first time at Hove.

An entertainment called *A Gipsy Phantasy* was held at Brooker Hall, 14 July 1915. The house was empty, but Mrs Vallance had agreed to open it for the occasion. The star of the show was her daughter-in-law, Mrs Claude Vallance, who sang beautifully 'Where My Caravan has Rested' and 'Little Grey Home in the West'.

ACKNOWLEDGEMENTS

The author would like to thank the following people and organizations for kindly loaning their photographs:

The late Dr Rex Binning, Mr C. Broadley, Miss Corscaden, East Sussex County Library, the Elphick family, Mr James Gray, the Graham Head Collection at the Cinema Museum, London (pages 48 & 49), Mrs R. Jackson, Mr Robert Jeeves of the Picture Postcard Saloon, Queen's Road, Brighton, Mr Ken Lane, Mr Barry Parks, Mr Gordon Renshawe, Mr R. Saunders, Mr Norman Shaw, Mr C. Snell, the late Miss Vivien Vallance.

I would also like to thank Michael Sullivan for copying the old photographs and Michael Horscroft for taking some of the recent photographs.

To order any of these titles please telephone our distributor, Littlehampton Book Services on 01903 72
For a catalogue of these and our other titles please ring Regina Schinner on 01453 731114